*"The pace and humor are good Gallico, the diction and diversions... Hemingway"* —Best Sellers

*Homer Smith is all man, topped off with a sense of humor and a singing heart . . .*

*Mother Maria Marthe is all nun, topped off with the disposition of a drill sergeant.*

*Together they achieve the impossible . . .*

**THE LILIES OF THE FIELD** was originally published by Doubleday and Company, Inc.

# THE LILIES

*Drawings by Burt Silverman*

POPULAR LIBRARY · NEW YORK

# OF THE FIELD
## By William E. Barrett

*All POPULAR LIBRARY books are carefully selected by the POPULAR LIBRARY Editorial Board and represent titles by the world's greatest authors.*

POPULAR LIBRARY EDITION
*Published in September, 1963*

*Copyright © 1962 by William E. Barrett*
*Library of Congress Catalog Card Number: 62-8085*

*Published by arrangement with Doubleday & Company, Inc.*
*Doubleday & Company edition published in April, 1962*
*Two printings*

*All of the characters in this book are fictitious, and any resemblance to actual persons, living or dead, is purely coincidental.*

PRINTED IN THE UNITED STATES OF AMERICA
*All Rights Reserved*

# THE
# LILIES
# OF
# THE
# FIELD

*For*
*My Godfather*
*David J. Groden*

## chapter one

There is a young legend developing on the west side of the mountains. It will, inevitably, grow with the years. Like all legends, it is composed of falsehood and fact. In this case, the truth is more compelling than the trappings of imagination with which it has been invested. The man who has become a legendary figure was, perhaps, of greater stature in simple reality than he ever will be in the oft-repeated, and expanded, tales which commemorate his deeds. Here, before the whole matter gets out of hand, is how it was. . . .

His name was Homer Smith. He was twenty-four. He stood six foot two and his skin was a deep, warm black. He had large, strong features and widely spaced eyes. A sculptor would have interpreted the features in terms of character, but Homer Smith's mother had once said of him that he was two parts amiable and one part plain devil. It was a verdict that he

*The Lilies of the Field*

accepted, as he accepted the days that came to him. He lived his life one day at a time. There was laughter in him.

He was a buck sergeant when he received his Army discharge at Fort Lewis. The Army years had been good to him and he had accumulated a sum of money through some slight thrift, much moonlighting and occasional gambling luck. He bought a secondhand station wagon in Seattle, equipped it for sleeping, and started out to see the West. He had not believed much of what he heard in the Army and he did not believe the tales that Westerners told about their country; he was, however, a curious man.

On a morning in May, Homer Smith drove into a valley west of the Rocky Mountain Range. Spring, which had stood aloof from him on the higher levels, moved down the valley to meet him. Blue, yellow, and pink flowers twinkled in the tawny expanse of buffalo and grama grass. He had grown up in South Carolina, a far different land from this. On his left, as he drove south, blue- and purple-tinted mountains tipped with snow formed a

*The Lilies of the Field*

seemingly unbroken barrier against the East, and everything that the East represented. In this country, he had discovered, there was no South; "south" was merely an adjective prefixed to the noun "west."

Where the road curved away from the mountains to parallel a narrow, sluggish stream, he saw the women. One of them was working in an area of cultivated land and three more were building a fence behind a dilapidated farmhouse. There were no men visible and that was curious. The women wore bulky-looking garments and they had white cloths tied, scarf fashion, around their heads. Homer appraised the house and the out-buildings with one glance.

"Place needs a lot of work," he said.

He hadn't worked for a week. It wasn't necessary that he work unless he felt the urge. In that fact lay a new concept of freedom. He was a man of many skills and when he became restless with idle traveling, he had no difficulty in finding work to do; when work became onerous, or the road called to him, he moved on. Impulse turned the wheel and he drove into the

*The Lilies of the Field*

badly rutted road which led to the farmhouse.

The woman in the field paused briefly to look toward the station wagon and so did the three women who were building a fence; a mere turning of heads, a brief pause before resuming the tasks which occupied them. The short, squat older woman who walked into the sunlight from the direction of the chicken run stood and watched Homer as he braked to a stop and slid from under the wheel. He chuckled in recognition of a familiar type. This was the sergeant, the top, the boss of these other women. No doubt about it.

"If you need a day's work done," he said cheerfully, "I'm for hire."

The woman had a hard, weather-beaten look. There were many deep lines on the broad surface of her face. Her eyes were small and sharply intent. She measured Homer before she spoke. She had a deep, guttural voice.

"*Gott ist gut*," she said. "He hass sent to me a big, stronk man."

Homer was intrigued by the heavy German accent, the careful spacing of words.

## The Lilies of the Field

He was amused, too, at the idea which the words conveyed.

"I dunno," he said. "He didn't say anything to me about sending me some place. I was just passing by."

"*Ja.* You did not pass."

There was aggressiveness in this old woman, an air of certainty which is the mark of bosses. Homer felt antagonism stir in him, but it was a fine day and he was carrying the day in his spirit. He had no quarrel with anyone. He waved one hand.

"I can build that fence better than those girls you've got," he said.

All of the lines in the woman's face seemed to draw together. He could see the effort that she was making to translate what he said in her own mind. He smiled reassuringly and strode away from her.

The three women had their fence half built, a high fence enclosing an area behind the house. Someone had dug postholes and spotted the posts in place. The women had fresh, unpainted planks and their method was for one woman to brace herself against the post, another to steady the plank, and the third to drive nails. All things consid-

## The Lilies of the Field

ered they were not doing badly. They stopped work, startled, when Homer's tall figure loomed over them. He gripped the post and shook it. It was a more solid job than he anticipated. The older woman was right behind him.

"*Nein!*" she said.

Her voice sputtered through three emphatic German sentences and he did not have to understand the words. She did not want him meddling with the fence. She had other work for him to do. He turned and the woman tapped herself on the chest. He caught the words, "Mutter Maria Marthe" which registered as a name. She indicated each of the three women in turn with a jabbing forefinger.

"Sister Elisabeth, Sister Gertrud, Sister Agnes."

"Religious folk," Homer thought. He nodded his head to each of them. "I'm real happy to meet you," he said. "I'm Homer Smith."

Mother Maria Marthe formed his name silently with her lips, then uttered it as it translated in her mind: "Homerus Schmidt."

*"Oh, ja!* Schmidt!"

Broad smiles broke across the faces of the three women. This was something that they could understand, a stranger named Schmidt. Their smiles made him welcome and Homer felt immediately at ease with them. They did not have any color line; he was just people to them. He made another attempt to do something about the fence but the harsh voice of the older woman stopped him at the first gesture.

"*Nein*, Schmidt," she said.

She pointed to the roof and delivered herself of another series of inexplicable sentences. Homer understood her without difficulty. This old woman was a natural boss and bosses always got their ideas across. She wanted the roof fixed.

"That's not something you do with Scotch tape and chewing gum," he said. "I'd need a good ladder and shingles, and the right kind of nails."

She made no effort to understand him; she merely anticipated him. With a purposeful stride, she led the way to the barn. There was a large room given over to tools and equipment. She had shingles, not

*The Lilies of the Field*

enough to reshingle a roof but enough to repair one that was not too far gone. She had nails of several sizes, including 3d flatheads. She had roofing cement. She had a ladder. Homer looked at her with respect. Here was a woman who knew what had to be done and what was needed to do it.

"Okay," he said. "I'll fix it good."

He was happy when he climbed the ladder and looked out over the valley. There was a chill in the wind but the sun was warm. He could see the three women working doggedly on their fence and, from his point of vantage, he could see what the fence enclosed. There was nothing in that little patch except a small statue and a privy.

"How about that?" he said softly. "All that work for just privacy. Away out here where there's nobody."

There was another privy north of the barn behind the foundation which marked the site of a house that had, obviously, burned down. This, he decided, was where the hired man had lived once, in a smaller house. It was curious that a fire would burn

*The Lilies of the Field*

a man's house down and leave his privy standing. It hardly seemed sensible.

He surveyed the roof carefully, aware from the markings that someone had surveyed it before him, indicating the places where it would have to be repaired. He was glad of that because a man couldn't tell from the outside where a wood shingle roof leaked, and he had not been invited inside. He wondered if the women would have done this job if he hadn't come along. Probably so. He looked down on the woman who was beating away at the fence planks with a hammer. It would be comical, he thought, to watch them on this roof beating on the shingles.

He worked while he amused himself thinking, rocking the broken and warped shingles to break them away from the hidden nails, sliding new shingles in place and nailing them, covering the nails with roofing cement. He worked swiftly, easily, finding the rhythm best suited to the job and maintaining it. He didn't count time and he was startled when a deep, heavy carrying voice called: "Schmidt!"

## The Lilies of the Field

Mother Maria Marthe was gesturing him down. The other women had already entered the house. The sun was directly overhead. Lunchtime. He scrambled down the ladder and slowed his pace as he approached the door of the house. There was a crucifix above the door; not a rugged Protestant cross but a crucifix. The word, "Catholic" came into his mind and with it the strange, awesome word, "nun." It had not occurred to him that these women were nuns. He found the idea incredible. What were they doing out here building fences?

They were standing in their places at a rough pine rectangular table that lacked a tablecloth, two on each side, Mother Maria Marthe at the head and a place for him, facing her. When he stood in his place, the older woman made the sign of the cross and the others followed her example. There was no doubt now. This was a Catholic place and these were nuns. Homer didn't join in the prayer and couldn't have done so if his Baptist conscience had permitted it. They prayed in German. It was a long prayer and, at a certain point, the

## The Lilies of the Field

rhythm changed as though something new had been added, something that wasn't in the memorized pattern. Homer was sensitive to rhythm. He was sensitive, too, to attitudes toward himself, a sensitivity born of race and skin color that set a man apart. He had delicate, invisible antennae which told him when he was noticed or discussed. He knew at the change in the prayer that these women were praying about him. The knowledge made him vaguely uncomfortable. Nobody was going to pray about getting a roof fixed, particularly a roof that wasn't in very bad shape. There had to be more to it than that.

"Amen" was the signal to be seated. Lunch consisted of thick cheese slices and coarse bread from a homemade loaf that was like a big, swollen pancake but solid. There was a glass of milk at each place; no coffee. Nobody talked and Homer studied the faces without staring at anybody. These were not young women, but two of them had a young look in spite of weather-roughened skin and tight dishtowel turbans that concealed their hair; Sister Gertrud who was the shortest nun,

## The Lilies of the Field

the one with the longest nose, and Sister Albertine who was frail-looking with large eyes, very blue. The other two, Sister Elisabeth and Sister Agnes, were sturdier and had broad faces. The eyes of Sister Elisabeth were brown.

Mother Maria Marthe presided grimly and it was obvious that no one was going to dawdle over lunch. All hands were going to eat in a hurry and go back to work. The sisters, seemingly, paid no attention to Homer Smith but he was aware of occasional hurried glances in his direction, and, more important to him, he felt friendliness. When he went back to his roof he was humming, and the hum grew to full song as he fell into the rhythm of the work. This was an interesting experience. The pay probably wouldn't be much. He didn't care. Maybe he wouldn't take any pay. He didn't know. Come night, he'd roll again.

In the pink of the evening, as he was cleaning the roof gutters, he saw Sister Agnes bringing in a cow, one cow in a country of herds. A few minutes later, as he gathered up his tools, he saw Mother

Maria Marthe emerge from the house, followed by Sisters Elisabeth and Gertrud who were carrying an Army cot. The older woman carried a bucket. He watched them, momentarily baffled, but when the toolroom in the barn became their obvious destination, he put all of the pieces of the puzzle together.

"They are doing that for me," he said. "Room and bath."

The idea touched him. A cot to sleep on and a bucket in which to wash! It was what they had. He swung down the ladder and followed them with long strides. They turned, startled, when they heard him. The two sisters held firmly to the cot. It was not Army, merely Army-type, the kind that are sold in surplus stores, collapsible and cheaply made.

"I didn't figure to stay," he said, "but I've got me a bed in the car."

Mother Maria Marthe did not understand him, so he gestured to the car and turned toward it. She followed him. The two sisters, after a moment of hesitation and lacking definite instructions, joined the procession, still carrying the cot. He

*The Lilies of the Field*

opened the station wagon from the rear and showed them the bed on which he slept. He had equipped that vehicle for living. He had his own bucket, too, a foot locker, a tool chest, and a guitar. The older nun nodded, then spoke to the other two in rapid-fire German. They started back to the house with the cot.

"*Das ist gut*, Schmidt," she said. "For zupper I rink a bell."

She walked away and Homer filled his bucket at the well, hauling it behind the barn for his wash-up. Supper was preceded by an even longer prayer than the one at lunch, and was only slightly more substantial as a meal. Sister Albertine served omelet with the coarse bread and a glass of milk. This was it; a house full of people living on the efforts of one cow and a few chickens. When another prayer had been said, two of the nuns made deft work of clearing away the dishes. There was a general air of relaxation. Sister Albertine, with badly concealed excitement, departed on a mysterious errand. Mother Maria Marthe sat less stiffly in her chair.

## The Lilies of the Field

"Ve are Cherman," she said, "mit two from Hungary. Ve learn der Englisch."

Sister Albertine returned with a small, tinny, wind-up model phonograph, the type that is bought for very young children. She placed a record on the turntable when the dishwashing nuns returned. A harsh, badly distorted voice squawked something in German from the speaker, followed by the English equivalent. The five voices repeated the English, including in the pronunciation all of the phonograph noises.

"Please send the valet up to my room," they said.

"I have something to be pressed."

"Do not starch the collars of the shirts."

"Here is my laundry list."

"Four shirts."

"Five pairs of socks."

"One blouse."

"Two pajamas."

Homer listened, fascinated and repelled. He had never been exposed to the problem of learning another language. He resented the voice on the record which wasted the

*The Lilies of the Field*

time of these people by teaching them to say stupid things. These nuns weren't ever going to see a valet, and they weren't going to have anything pressed. He had an expressive face and Mother Maria Marthe read it when the pause at the end of the record occurred. She halted Sister Albertine who was about to turn the record over.

"Vait!" she said. "Schmidt! He spiks der Englisch."

Homer sat suspended in the sudden hush, aware of the eyes. He was, suddenly, elevated above his status as a big, strong man, above the disembodied voice on the record. Sister Albertine was so carried away that she spoke without waiting for permission. She pointed to the phonograph.

"Vot iss named this?" she said.

"A phonograph."

Homer's reply broke down discipline. If Sister Albertine could ask a question so could anyone else. Each nun was indicating some object in the room. He named them as rapidly as he could, trying to speak the words distinctly. He could tell from their delighted expressions that they already knew the words "table," "chair," "window," "door," and the words for the other familiar objects. His identification pleased them by confirming what they knew. Mother Maria Marthe put a stop to the obvious. She went through the pantomime of shaking hands with one of the nuns and he told her what she was doing, pointing out the "you" and the "her." He became self-conscious about the South Carolina in his voice.

"If you learn English from me," he said apologetically, "you're sure enough going to get yourselves segregated some places."

They looked at him uncomprehendingly and he let the subject drop. That was something that he could not explain even to himself. Sister Albertine was drawing a sketch on a piece of paper. She showed it to him. It was a very good sketch of his station wagon.

"Automobile? No?" she said. "Auto bus, no?"

She knew that it had a special name and she did better with English than did the others. They were all interested but when he told them that it was a station

*The Lilies of the Field*

wagon, he drew blank looks. With a few deft strokes, the nun drew a depot, then a wagon. This was a station and this, a wagon. How could you put them together and obtain something that resembled an automobile?

He did not explain that very well, but he tried. He was sorry when Mother Maria Marthe clapped her hands as a signal that class was over. He walked to his home on wheels in the cool darkness, with a thousand stars swung low above him and his brain filled with strange rhythms; German words and English words flavored with German. He did not ask himself why he was spending the night; he was here and it happened. He wondered which of the nuns would have slept on the floor and managed without a bucket if he hadn't had his own equipment.

These nuns are nice people, he thought, and that old lady's got a shrewd mind, loose and easy.

*chapter two*

One of the privileges of freedom was that a man slept until he felt like rising, with no bugles blowing. Homer Smith was not a late sleeper but he did not believe in stumbling around in half light, waking up birds. The morning was nicely lighted in the sky when he rose, filled his bucket at the well and hauled it beyond the barn. There was a hammer hammering and, from the corners of his eyes, he could see Mother Maria Marthe watching him while he was filling his bucket. She did not bother him until he came back to the station wagon; then she descended angrily.

"Schmidt!" Her words tumbled out and they were so German, or so German-English, that they were incomprehensible. She did not, however, need words to convey meaning; she needed only gestures and emphasis. The gist of the message was plain. He was a lazy loafer who had no business sacking out when there was work to be done. Homer drew himself up, looking at her from his commanding height, as angry as she was.

"Look!" he said. "I ain't no nun and I ain't no hired hand, neither. I get up when I feel like getting up. If I don't want to work, I don't work."

He did not awe her. She stamped her foot, pointing emphatically at the house. "*Geh!*" she said. "*Mach schnell!*"

Being commanded to go to the house meant that he was expected to eat breakfast. That was an idea that made sense. He turned away, still angry. Sister Albertine greeted him shyly in the communal dining room. She had, obviously, been forced to waste her time preparing a late breakfast for him and she was nervous about it. She set two fried eggs before him, following them with two slabs of coarse bread, toasted. There was no coffee, only the inevitable milk.

"Old Mother sure sets a poor table," Homer said. "How come she can afford all that lumber outside and no money for chow?"

Sister Albertine stared at him, her large

eyes seeming larger still as she tried to understand him. Homer didn't expect her to understand him. It was a comfort to him to express his feelings in words with a human audience to listen to him; he did not require a response.

"There's a mean streak in that old woman," he said. "I don't know why you girls put up with her. People got to sleep. People got to eat. People got to have a little joy in living. She don't go for that. All this milk all the time and no coffee! And no milk of human kindness, neither. That woman just hasn't got it."

Sister Albertine gestured helplessly. "I do not understand," she said. "Speak slowly please."

Her English sounded like English, or more like English than Mother Maria Marthe's, even if she did speak one word at a time.

"I'm going to give you some soup," he said. "Got some soup in the car. Emergency rations. Got a can of peaches, too. You wait right here! I'll bring them right in."

Sister Albertine looked frightened but

## The Lilies of the Field

there was one note in the human voice that she understood, the note of command. She nodded her head weakly and started clearing the dishes from the table. Homer strode out to the station wagon.

"I hope Old Mother tries to stop me," he said. "Just let her ask me what I'm doing."

He was in a high, exalted mood, flying the flags of rebellion against authority. No one attempted to stop him and he took five cans of soup out of his locker, a can of peaches, a can opener. He saw Mother Maria Marthe bearing down on him as he started back to the house and his flags drooped on the flagstaff. He pretended that he did not see her and lengthened his stride. He piled his cans on the table, resisting the impulse to look over his shoulder. He went through the pantomime of opening the cans for the benefit of Sister Albertine.

"Soup," he said.

"*Ja.* Thank you."

She looked interested, but she also looked fearful. She did not have the authority to accept gifts, but she lacked the

*The Lilies of the Field*

vocabulary necessary to refuse acceptance or to explain her dilemma. Homer sensed it.

"Old Mother will like that soup," he said. "Save a little wear and tear on that cow and those chickens."

He went out to face the dragon and the dragon was waiting for him. "Schmidt," Mother Maria Marthe said, "Ve build a shapel. I show you."

She led the way with firm tread to the old foundation over which a house had burned. Coarse grasses had grown around it and the foundation itself was a pit into which ash and brick and partially consumed timbers had fallen. She reached into her pocket and produced a sketch on a piece of coarse wrapping paper. It was a good sketch of a small church, a frame church that looked like many Baptist churches in the South except that it did not have a steeple. There was a cross on the first roof truss above the door.

"Who builds it?" he said.

Her eyes drilled into him. She was patient and she could wait upon the perception of a dull-witted male. Homer looked

*The Lilies of the Field*

from the unsightly foundation to the sketch and back again. There was a pile of new lumber behind the barn.

"If you think that I'm building that, you're out of your mind," he said. "I'm one man. I ain't no contractor with a crew. I don't need all that work, neither." He handed the sketch back to her. "No."

There was hard-eyed contempt in the old woman's face. She folded the sketch into a hidden pocket. "Ve are vimmen," she said. "Ve build it."

"All right. You build it."

Anger boiled and bubbled in Homer Smith. He could feel the steam from it rising into his brain. He looked away from Mother Maria Marthe and it helped to bring his anger down to a simmer, not looking at her. She was a mean-minded, overriding, unreasonable old woman. He was going to get in his station wagon and drive. The warmth of the day touched his skin and he was looking toward the debris in the foundation. He had had his breakfast. Breakfast sort of committed a man to the day. He felt strongly about people passing judgment on him and he did not

*The Lilies of the Field*

want this woman justified in thinking ill of him.

"I'll clean that old foundation for you before I go," he said.

He walked away from her, tall in his pride. There was a scoop shovel in the toolhouse and, surprisingly, a crowbar. He had a spade in his car. He came back and surveyed the ruin of a house. The builder had put down a solid foundation of granite. Not many farmhouses in this section of country were built like this. It made sense. A man had to have a cool place for his perishable stuff. The big house where the nuns lived was probably built the same way. The chimney stood above the foundation, tall and built of brick, a lonely thing without a house to keep it company.

"Strange how it burned the man's house and left his privy."

Homer shook his head over the familiar thought as he surveyed the ruin. The years had fallen on the grave of that house; snows and rains and blowing sand. The debris was packed into the pit and it looked like a town dump set in cement. A bulldozer would churn it up fast. He knew

*The Lilies of the Field*

how to handle a bulldozer, but this was a place of hungry labor where a man was lucky because he had a shovel and a crowbar. Resentment against Mother Maria Marthe moved hotly in him again. He paced off the dimensions of the foundation, confirming what his eye told him. It was 18 × 26.

He dropped down into the pit and started probing. It had been a hot fire and the house had probably gone fast. Some of the lumber had survived, charred but not burned through. Someone had started the cleaning-out process long ago and quit. It was impossible to tell how that fire had gone. It probably smothered out some way. Maybe it happened in the winter and the snow came. There weren't any clues left to show what had happened to the roof. He did not believe that it had been reduced to ash.

"Old farmer took him some salvage," he said. "Hauled away what would haul."

He was encouraged when he discovered that the burned lumber moved against his pry. It had partially roofed the excavation. This hole wasn't as solidly packed as it

*The Lilies of the Field*

looked. Fire-eaten though they were, the lumbers were heavy and he strained his muscles against them, heaving them out. His body absorbed thought and emotion, condensing them into sweat. When he heard a bell ringing in the distance he did not immediately translate it into meaning.

"Old Mother going to feed the slaves," he said.

Resentment returned. He was filthy. Clouds of black ash rose from his work clothes when he slapped them. He went to the station wagon for his bucket and washed in cold water from the well, accepting the icy touch of it gratefully. The nuns were standing in their places at the table, waiting for him before starting their prayers. He didn't say Catholic prayers with them but he had to be there. It was some idea in Old Mother's mind. He bowed his head. He had a prayer in his own heart when he accepted food. Nobody took food for granted when he was a child. It wasn't always easy to get and a person learned to be thankful when it was there.

He sat down at the table and there were soup plates at each place. Sister Albertine

*The Lilies of the Field*

came in with a pot and a ladle. She looked happy. All the nuns looked happy. Mother Maria Marthe didn't look exactly happy but she didn't look as stern as usual. Homer's mood lifted. They were serving his soup.

Nobody talked. That seemed to be the rule at lunchtime. Still, without talking, it was a pleasant meal. Nice atmosphere. These girls, Homer thought, need better food. He wished that he had more cans in his car. He didn't feel full-fed when he rose but his stomach was friendly to him. When a man felt welcome at a table the food tasted better.

He was whistling when he returned to the excavation. He stood with his hands in his pockets looking at it. Old Mother, he repeated to himself, was out of her mind. Nobody could build a church like her drawing unless he was a contractor with people working for him, people skilled in doing different things. Women weren't ever going to build it, especially not women that built a fence so clumsy. All of which made cleaning out all of this mess ridiculous. He had told her that he'd clean

## The Lilies of the Field

it out before he left, however, and he'd do it.

He was a strong man and the work went fast when he didn't think about it. He got all of the odds and ends of wood and metal out of the hole, then worked them into a trench about a dozen yards away. He cleaned the stone steps that had led into the cellar from the outside, but the cellar was deep. A man could walk around in it with the top of his head under ground. Getting out the ash and the sand was not mere shoveling; it was hauling. He did not want to use his own pail so he rummaged around in the barn until he found a bucket that had seen hard service. After that, monotony claimed him; shoveling, filling, carrying out, and dumping.

He created a refuse pile that would have to be leveled off some day but he had no alternative and it did not worry him. Blue dusk came down on an uncompleted job and his muscles ached. The distant bell rang again.

They were back to eggs for the evening meal. The eggs irritated him. He was tired and hungry and he'd spent his day doing

*The Lilies of the Field*

a job that didn't add up to anything. There wasn't enough food to satisfy him and Mother Maria Marthe sat stiffly at the head of the table keeping everything on a low key. She never said a word of thanks to anybody for anything.

"I'm going to get me my pay and leave."

The resolve sustained him, even when he was swept into an English lesson after dinner. The nuns, he discovered, had been studying English, not merely trying to learn it from a phonograph record. They brought their books with them and they knew many English words. Their problem was that they never heard anyone speak those words and they had no practice in speaking them. Homer was not in a mood for teaching anybody anything and he gave their problem only half his mind. He could feel the disappointment of the nuns but he was concentrating on the boss nun and he couldn't give any thought to the others. When Mother Maria Marthe clapped her hands at the conclusion of the lesson, he braced himself.

"I want to talk to you," he said. "I've

*The Lilies of the Field*

been doing work for you. Good work. I want pay for what I do."

She sat silent, with her hands clasped in front of her. Her small eyes looked at him out of the wrinkled mask of her face but there was no light in them. He did not know whether she understood him or not; if she did, she would not admit it. She could make a person feel wrong, like a miserable sinner, by just looking at him. If she refused to cross over into English, he couldn't talk to her. He looked past her to the little table under the statue of the Mother of Jesus in the corner of the room. There was a book on the table, a big book, and it talked to him. The Bible! He crossed the room and looked at it, turning a few pages. The type was outlandish and did not look like words, but no other book was organized like this one.

"You wait right here," he said. "I'm coming back."

He was afraid that she would not wait, that she would close the door on him; but she waited. He brought his own Bible from the station wagon. It was the one he got

*The Lilies of the Field*

in the Army. He had a passage in his mind and he turned pages rapidly. He tore half of the wrapping from a package of cigarettes and wrote on the white side, *Luke 10:7.*

Mother Maria Marthe rose heavily and crossed the room to her big Bible. She turned the pages and he knew what she was reading when the page-turning stopped:

"And in the same house remain, eating and drinking such things as they give: for the labourer is worthy of his hire."

It wasn't exactly what he wanted to say, but he hoped that she would get the idea about the laborer. She walked slowly back and reached for his pencil. In bold letters, she wrote, *Proverbs 1:14.*

He spun his own pages and read: "Cast in thy lot among us: let us all have one purse."

"No," he said. "I'm a poor man. I have to work for wages."

Mother Maria Marthe did not change expression. Without returning to consult her Bible, she wrote again on the fragment of cigarette package, *Matthew 6:28, 29.*

*The Lilies of the Field*

"And why take ye thought for raiment? Consider the lilies of the field, how they grow; they toil not, neither do they spin."

"And yet I say unto you. That even Solomon in all his glory was not arrayed like one of these."

Homer read, baffled. This old woman had answers out of the Book, which surprised him. They did not come to grips with the situation, they did not deal directly with his right to be paid, but they slowed down a man in argument. Before he went into the Army, he had had a head filled with Bible words and figures but they would not march straight for him now as they did once. It wouldn't make any difference. This old woman wasn't going to pay him. She'd never had any intention of paying him. She sat straight with her unblinking eyes fixed on his face.

"Schmidt," she said. "Tomorrow Sunday ist. Der Mass in Piedras iss nine by der clock."

"I don't go to Mass."

"Ve do."

She sat immovable, letting the statement stand in all finality until his comprehension

*The Lilies of the Field*

caught up with it. She expected him to drive the nuns to Mass.

"How did you get there before I came?" he said.

"Ve valked."

That, too, had finality in it, completeness. Piedras was a little town. Homer had driven through it before he stopped here. It was over two miles away. He thought about those nuns, working hard all day on thin rations, walking miles along the road on Sunday. He liked those nuns. It wasn't fair to them.

"I'll drive you in," he said.

He walked out, then; not expecting thanks and not wanting any. A man was free when he could say "yes" or say "no." Old Mother had her ways and she was a tricky woman but she hadn't asked him to take her to Mass. He had to be honest about it; she hadn't asked him that. That wasn't her way. She put a problem up to a man. She knew how to set a problem up for him so there wasn't anything he could do but take it from her.

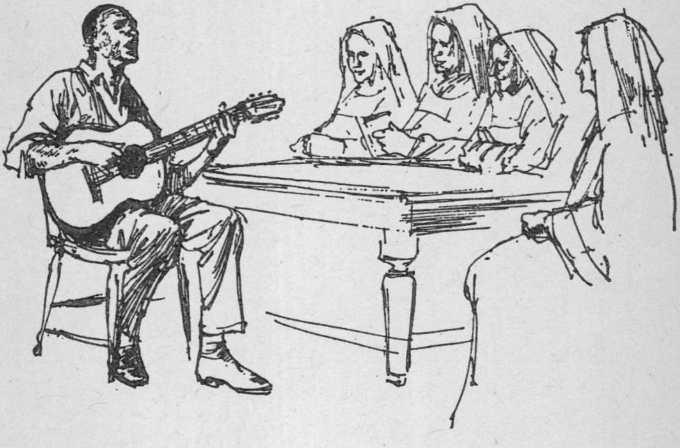

## chapter three

The morning was still, with no movement in the wide and lonely land. Homer Smith rose early. He dressed in a pair of Army slacks, a button-down gray shirt, a blue necktie, a gray jacket. A man had to look sharp on Sunday if no other time. He wandered around aimlessly, missing the sense of life, movement and activity that he associated with this strange place in which he found himself. As time passed, with no bell sounding, it became apparent that there would be no breakfast. He remembered vaguely from the Army that Catholics, or some Catholics, did not have breakfast before Mass. His own hunger was the captive of Catholic custom and he was uncomfortable. He removed his bed from the station wagon, providing space if not comfort for his passengers. At 8:30 they emerged.

Mother Maria Marthe and her four nuns wore long black robes with white starched

## The Lilies of the Field

bibs and white bands across their foreheads under black hoods. They looked now like his idea of nuns but he was astonished at them.

"You girls sure look nice," he said.

Whether they understood his English or not, they recognized a compliment by its tone. They looked pleased. Mother Maria Marthe wasted no time on looking pleased. She sized up the station wagon, ordered the nuns into the back and elected to ride with the driver. There were no seats in the back so the passengers sat on the floor. There was something pleasant and companionable about that and Homer had an impulse to sing as he drove out onto the road. He didn't sing. The stiff, no-nonsense woman beside him wouldn't put in with singing. He was certain of that.

Piedras was a shabby little town and the church was a flat-roofed structure of adobe. Homer let his passengers out and stood beside the station wagon, ignoring the hard stare of Old Mother. This close was as close as he intended to go to a Catholic Mass. He waited until the nuns entered the church, then crossed the street. There

*The Lilies of the Field*

were signs in Spanish all over the windows of a small café and he did not have to understand Spanish to recognize a place that sold beer and miscellaneous food. He wasn't certain that it would be open, but it was. A thin man with sad brown eyes rose from a stool and moved behind the counter.

"I want a man's breakfast," Homer said. "Ham and eggs, with lots of ham, and pancakes, and anything else you've got, and coffee. I want lots of coffee and I start with it."

"*Sí*. I can do it. You are the man who does the work for those nuns?"

"They do a lot of work themselves."

"*Sí*. This I know. It is a great folly. They cannot make the living in this country. It is not possible."

A steaming cup of coffee appeared on the counter in front of Homer and he inhaled the fragrance of it. The sad man had a grill behind the counter and he broke eggs onto it. Ham sizzled and Homer's nostrils twitched. He hadn't ever thought about nuns making a living. New thoughts interested him.

"They are Germans. They speak the

*The Lilies of the Field*

good Spanish but nobody listens. There is no reason for it."

The little man talked on. He knew all about the nuns, or claimed that he did. They were from the wrong Germany, "the one that is Communist," and they escaped, which was a great embarrassment to their Order. But yes. There was some politics about it which no one could understand. "It is Church politics and politics of Europe, and who can understand the politics even when it is of his own country?" The nuns could not stay in Germany and the Order owned this land. It came to them in the will of Gus Ritter. Did the customer know Gus Ritter?

Everybody in this place knew him; *todo el mundo*. He was a hard, mean man who worked his family night and day to make money for him. His son and his son's wife burned to death in the house next to him. A lamp of kerosene caused it. He was too mean, Gus Ritter, to have electricity although poor people in this country had it. After his son burned up, he did not live long. He left his land to this Order of nuns because his sister in Germany belonged to

## The Lilies of the Field

it. For a long time the land was idle. Gus Ritter made good money from it growing the potato. These nuns came and they had nothing. They knew nothing except to teach. There was no school and they did not know the English. How could they teach? They sold some land to buy tools and furniture and lumber. For what purpose? What could they do? Would the customer have some more of the eggs?

The customer wasn't interested in eggs but he would have more ham. Homer Smith was enjoying this experience. He was catching up on his victuals after two lean days. The steady flow of talk from behind the counter fascinated him. He had always had a weakness for good talkers. He liked the cadences which Spanish brought to English and the occasional Spanish words or phrases, meaning nothing, delighted him because they so obviously belonged to what the man was trying to say.

"The Mass is finish," the man said.

There were a few people coming out of the church across the street. Homer rose and stretched. It had been a noble breakfast. As he was paying for it, he thought

*The Lilies of the Field*

about those hungry nuns. He hesitated. Working only occasionally and traveling much, he had learned thrift. He shrugged and purchased five slices of ham which he carried to the car in a paper sack.

The main body of worshipers moved slowly out of the church; Spanish, all of them. Poor people. Homer towered above them as he stood beside his station wagon and he was aware of his physical superiority as he was aware of the curious glances that he attracted. Nobody spoke to him.

The nuns did not come out until after everyone else had gone. The priest came with them, a short, thin man in a brown robe with a white cord around his waist. Mother Maria Marthe was talking to him in Spanish. Her Spanish did not have a lot of German in it like her English did. She introduced Homer to the priest and he did not understand what she said about him, but he caught his own name. She called him "Señor Schmidt." Señor means "mister" in Spanish. He knew that. She never called him mister in English. The priest was Father Gomez. These Catholics were a comical people. They called themselves

*The Lilies of the Field*

"Father" and "Mother" when they weren't and when they didn't aim to be.

The priest shook hands with him. He was a quiet man, half sad like all these Spanish, with a low voice. He wouldn't be likely to get a call from a Baptist church. He wasn't an exhorting type. He said something nice about Homer being good to the nuns.

"Mother Superior tells me that you are going to build her a chapel," he said.

"That is just an idea she's got in her head. One man can't do that."

Homer felt embarrassed when he read disappointment in the priest's eyes. He had no reason to feel embarrassed but he did. He spoke hurriedly to cover what he felt.

"I been studying your church. Never saw one like it before. Not close up."

"It is not impressive but I would like to show it to you."

The priest brightened. He led Homer to the wall of the church and showed him where the outside coating of adobe had cracked. There were adobe bricks underneath. "They are simple bricks," he said. "They are made out of adobe clay and a

*The Lilies of the Field*

little straw, sometimes the manure of the horse, then dried in the sun."

The door was of rough board. Homer hesitated when the priest opened it. He had never been inside a Catholic church. There were vague memories in his mind about tales he had heard of weird Catholic spells and of idol worship, but he was curious about the construction of the building so he followed the priest in. There was an altar and there were rows of rough benches, strange-looking images that wore clothes, murals of Biblical scenes painted on the walls. The walls were whitewashed adobe, concealing the brickwork. There was a poverty about it that attracted Homer Smith. He understood poverty.

The priest was telling him that he had three other churches like this one in which he said Mass on Sundays, that his home parish was in the larger town of North Fork. Homer nodded. This was a busy man, a circuit-riding preacher. He respected him.

"I'm glad I saw your church," he said.

"It is a poor church but God comes down to it." The priest's eyes were intent

## The Lilies of the Field

upon Homer's face. "Mother Superior says that she prayed for someone to help her and that you came. What do you think about that?"

Homer laughed. He did not mean to laugh but this was a disturbing subject. "I think that she figures that she owns me. She figures that the Lord gave me to her as a present because she did all that praying."

"Not that!" the priest said. "I am certain, not that. But she has a need and she trusted in prayer. It is not a fault in her if she believes that God sent you."

"He didn't send a black Baptist to a Catholic nun. He didn't do anything like that."

"It would be odd, wouldn't it?"

"I don't see much sense in what she's doing."

"She does what she must at the present. These nuns have to live. She wants a place here ultimately for poor boys from the city; Spanish-speaking boys who get into trouble. No one is interested in them. They could work and learn and be happier in the country than in the city. No one will believe that until she proves it. She knows

*The Lilies of the Field*

what she wants to do and she is strong of will."

"Yes," Homer said. "I know that. She's a strong-minded woman. But God didn't give me to her and she doesn't own me. She's got to get that out of her head."

He was thoughtful driving home and he declined the breakfast invitation, abrupt in his presentation of the paper sack to Mother Maria Marthe. "Just a little ham," he said. "Maybe you girls might like it."

He gave her no opportunity to say thanks or not to say thanks. He turned away hurriedly and climbed into the station wagon. He drove to a parking place close to the excavation and changed into his working clothes. He had an innate respect for the Sabbath and a disinclination to profane it with servile work, but the Army had relaxed the rigid rules of his boyhood. In the Army a job that had to be done on Sunday was done on Sunday. It was like the ass or the ox falling into a pit and having to be hauled out. The nuns, however, seemed to be abiding by the old rules so he restrained his urge to plunge in and finish the clearing of the excavation.

## The Lilies of the Field

He walked around the excavation and measured it again. He returned to the station wagon and obtained a small pad from his locker. He covered the pad with figures. He had worked for many people and he had done many things. He had varied skills. Always he had worked with someone telling him what to do. Nobody, in all of his life before this, had told him to build a church. Nobody had ever said to him: "Here is the ground and here I want a church and it is your job to build it." It was like a call. It elevated him. He was all alone, one man, with a hole in the ground and a church to be built, and no one to tell him how.

He took his black pipe from his locker and packed it. He smoked cigarettes during the week, but on Sunday he smoked a pipe. It was his father's habit. His father could not afford to smoke tobacco seven days a week, so he settled for Sunday. Homer had been smoking a black pipe like his father's on Sunday ever since his father died. In his mind it was sort of a memorial and he drew satisfaction from it.

He sat on the small pile of partly con-

## The Lilies of the Field

sumed lumber that he had stacked a few yards away from the foundation. He puffed on his pipe and there was a sheen over his eyes. He was seeing something before him that wasn't there and the world around him did not exist. He was unaware of Mother Maria Marthe until she spread the wide skirts of her black robe and sat beside him on the lumber. It was the most companionable thing that she had ever done.

"Schmidt," she said, "ve can do it?"

It wasn't a statement; it was a question. That, too, was unusual, but Homer's mind was away out where the unusual is usual and nothing ordinary matters.

"It would take a powerful lot of work," he said, "and a lot of those 'dobe bricks."

"How much?"

"About the work, I don't know. Nearly four thousand bricks."

They sat silent, contemplating the foundation where once a house had stood and where a man and woman had burned to death. Mother Maria Marthe rose.

"Tomorrow ve go to North Fork," she said.

*The Lilies of the Field*

Homer didn't answer. North Fork was the big town of this section. He hadn't seen it yet. If she wanted to go, he'd take her. She wouldn't do anything about the gasoline. Gasoline was like the lilies of the field to her; somehow it would be provided.

The noon heat pressed down and he moved into the shade of the station wagon. The land was big and there was loneliness all around him. He thought about going back to Piedras and listening to the Spanish man at the eating place, but that was too much trouble. The day, without work or travel, seemed as big and as empty as the country. He took his guitar out of the station wagon. He traveled with everything that he liked in that old vehicle because it was his home while he rambled. He had bought the guitar in a pawnshop in Tacoma, a better instrument than the one he had owned back in South Carolina. He tuned it and played softly, feeling his way into a mood. In a little while he was singing, keeping his voice down, not putting out anything, singing to his own soul.

He sang "Wade in the Water" and "Deep River," "Blind Barnabas" and "Old

*The Lilies of the Field*

Time Religion." He let his voice swell out a little on "Shenandoah" because, suddenly the mood was right and the song was saying what he felt inside of him. Mother Maria Marthe returned then and he felt her presence without seeing her. His mood was stronger than her presence and his voice made its last crossing of the wide Missouri before he looked up. The old face, with its deeply graven wrinkles, was forbidding but the small eyes seemed less hard than usual.

"Schmidt," she said. "Come! Brink der music."

He rose reluctantly to follow her. He had been doing all right alone. His resentment melted when he saw the four nuns waiting expectantly in the dining room. The table had been pushed back and his chair was placed so that he would face them. They were women without music in a great, flat, lonely place that was intolerable without it. He looked at them and his heart lifted. These were people who needed something that he had to give.

He started softly, offering religion to religious people; "Swing Low, Sweet Char-

*The Lilies of the Field*

iot" and "Didn't My Lord Deliver Daniel." He warmed to them, then, and worked to lift them, swinging into: "Ezekiel Saw the Wheel" and "Dry Bones." Their feet moved and their eyes were alive. Old Mother sitting stiffly, didn't seem to mind, so he did "Water Boy" and "John Henry." He had no particular awareness of his voice except as an instrument like his guitar. It was deep, a bass-baritone, and he could do with a song whatever he felt like doing at the moment, but he did not try to make his voice obey any rules. When he finished "John Henry," Mother Maria Marthe clapped her hands. It wasn't applause; it was the end of his solo.

"Ve sing," she said.

He nodded, accepting the role of accompanist. "Give me the key," he said, "and let us hear how it goes."

The old nun nodded to Sister Albertine who had a moment of shyness. She wet her lips and her thin fingers tightened, making fists out of her hands. Her large blue eyes met Homer's and she leaned forward. She sang and her voice was true, a sweet voice, not strong but perfectly pitched. A man

*The Lilies of the Field*

could follow it. Homer watched her and listened to her, tuning the guitar. What she was doing was chant, a simple thing. He drew deep organ sounds from the guitar and it was right. Everything was right; the voice, the music, the accompaniment. Sister Albertine felt him with her and she signaled to the others. They came in and they knew what they were doing. None of the voices was as good as Sister Albertine's but this chant did not call for good voices. Sister Gertrud's voice was harsh. Sisters Agnes and Elisabeth sounded like just anybody out of a Baptist choir, and the old Mother's voice was cracked; but, together, they made a strange, solemn sense.

This was Latin. It was Homer's first experience with sung Latin and he approved the sound of it. It belonged to this music. As they changed from one hymn to another, Sister Albertine led him into the sense of the new chant and the others joined in as he picked it up. Loneliness had long since dropped away from him and he felt exultation. He wanted to mingle his voice with these others but the words

*The Lilies of the Field*

eluded him so long as he regarded them as words; when he thought of them merely as sounds, they made a pattern in his mind. He signaled to Sister Albertine for a repeat at one point and when he heard the sounds a second time they clung to his mind. The voices of the nuns came in again and his voice joined them.

*Ave maris stella*
*Dei mater alma*
*Atque semper virgo*
*Felix coeli porta.*

It was that easy. They stopped when Mother Maria Marthe clapped her hands. It was suppertime but Homer paid no attention to his food. He ate it but it made no impression on him. When he walked to the station wagon, he was empty of thought but filled with throbbing sound, a happy feeling of reverence. He stood for a long time looking at the shadowed shape of the excavation.

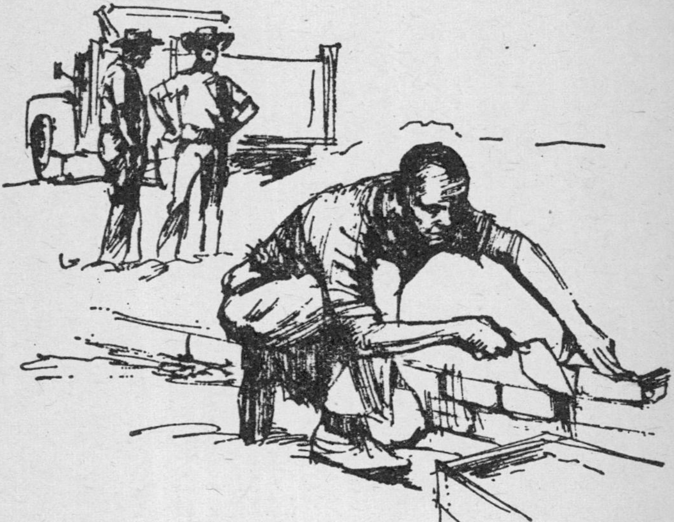

## chapter four

North Fork had a population of 7094 people, which made it the metropolis of the west slope where towns were small and widely spaced. It was a spread-out town and the Livingston Construction Company was on the northern outskirts. Mother Maria Marthe was accompanied by Sister Gertrud. The two nuns left Homer Smith beside the station wagon while they entered the Livingston office. Homer lighted a cigarette and looked at the construction company property with interest. He had no idea why old Mother was visiting this place but it had a prosperous look.

Politician, this man, Livingston, he decided.

There were several earth-moving machines standing in a row and spaces indicating that there were others out on a job. There were four good-sized buildings and an adjoining lumber yard. All of which, on this side of the mountains, added up to

*The Lilies of the Field*

road-building contracts and government work. A man didn't employ such equipment out in the wide open spaces by merely hanging out a sign or putting an ad in the paper.

Rolling in it, Homer thought. This man is doing all right.

He was idly curious about Mother Maria Marthe's mission but speculation never engaged his mind for long. He either knew something or he didn't know, found out ultimately or never found out. He walked around, admiring the equipment. He had resumed his post beside the station wagon when a short, firm-jawed, gray-haired man exited briskly from the office door. The man seemed angry, either temporarily or permanently so. He looked at Homer challengingly, looked past him, then met his eyes.

"Are you Schmidt?" he said incredulously.

"That's a German idea," Homer said softly. "My folks figured that it was Smith. Named me Homer."

"You're the man who is going to build a chapel for those nuns?"

*The Lilies of the Field*

Homer was about to say that that was another German idea, one of old Mother's ideas, but he didn't like the man's attitude. The man didn't seek information in a polite and orderly way.

"Yes," he said.

"I expected a different type. Hell! You'll never do it."

Homer kept his eyes on the other man's face; not answering, merely waiting. This was an attitude that he understood although he had not encountered it lately. This man expected to meet somebody white; when he discovered that he was dealing with a Negro, he "knew" that the job wouldn't be done. A voice inside Homer said: "The man's right. You know he's right. You won't do it." He closed the voice out, refusing to listen.

"I'm Orville Livingston," the man said. "I don't know how you got mixed up in this, but I told this nun when she first came here that she'd better go back again. I was Gus Ritter's friend and the executor of his estate. I turned his property over to this religious Order, which was what he wanted. I sold land for those nuns after

*The Lilies of the Field*

they came here, without taking a commission. I had a man plow for them when they insisted on working the land that they kept, and I paid him personally. Now they want bricks. I've got to stop somewhere. I'm a Methodist."

"I'm a Baptist myself."

"You are? Then why are you working for them? If you are?"

"I haven't figured that out yet."

"You'll figure it out. Then you'll quit. Those nuns will figure it out, too; figure out that what people told them was right. Then they'll quit. They must. Women can't work that land and if their Church was interested in them, it wouldn't leave them out here. They'll quit and anything that they start will fall to ruin."

"Old Mother has a strong idea in her mind," Homer said softly. "She's going to do what she feels she must."

"Certainly. If somebody else supplies the bricks! Well, I won't. I wanted to see you before I told her."

Orville Livingston did not seem to realize that he had made Homer Smith the last toppling weight in the scales of deci-

*The Lilies of the Field*

sion against the nuns, and that he was telling him so.

"You've got that right," Homer said. "I can't talk against you on that. I'm still doing that job for them. I'm going to need two days work a week to keep it going. I can handle a bulldozer, almost any machinery you've got. Learned how in the Army."

"All right. I can use you Thursday and Friday if you can only work two days. I'll pay the going rate on whatever job you're assigned. Seven Thursday morning. I'll try you out."

Orville Livingston turned away. "Another thing," Homer said, "I'll need two sacks of cement. For them I'll pay cash."

"Three dollars. I'll have a man wheel them out."

Homer lighted another cigarette. Something had happened to him. He didn't plan any part of it. He had taken a job that he didn't want under a man whom he didn't like and he'd told the man that he was going to build a church. It didn't make sense. He stared across the big lot of the Livingston Construction Company, seeing

## The Lilies of the Field

none of it, seeking in his mind for a way out of a worrisome situation. A sentence kept repeating itself like an outside voice speaking to him; *"I expected a different type."* Then, another sentence; *"I wanted to see you before I told her."* He'd let old Mother down merely by being black.

A man wheeled out two sacks of cement and Homer paid for them. They weighed 94 pounds a sack and he heaved them into the back of the station wagon. His muscles felt good doing it.

The two nuns emerged from the office and any sentimental feeling that he had developed for Mother Maria Marthe vanished immediately. She was in bad humor.

"Schmidt," she said curtly, "ve go back."

"No, we don't. I've got things to do."

His pride stood tall, contradicting her and not explaining anything. The two nuns were riding in the front with him because there was no sensible alternative. He could hear the old nun breathing heavily.

"Ve haff no time," she said.

He ignored her and drove downtown. North Fork had a variety of stores concentrated on two streets. He found the town interesting after a period of isolation. He bought a spirit level and a couple of good saws, a heavy hammer, a chisel, and a hoe with a ventilated blade. The expenditure dismayed him but he assured himself that he would pay the money back to his fund out of his pay on Friday. He couldn't afford a big investment in something that probably wasn't going to get done.

"Schmidt," Mother Maria Marthe said when they were halfway home, "ve haff no bricks."

"We'll get some."

He didn't know where or how, but that was a problem of the future and the future was never quite real to him. A man couldn't calculate on time that hadn't arrived, happenings that hadn't happened; he had all that he could do in coping with what was already here. The here and the now of this afternoon was the finishing of the foundation clean-out. It took his afternoon and part of the next day. He built a mortar box, got a level on the foundation, chiseled off the rough spots and mixed cement. He started on the task of smoothing the top of the foundation with cement and he

*The Lilies of the Field*

worked carefully, missing the direction of a boss while savoring the joy of being his own man with a job that was his to plan and to execute. On Thursday and Friday he worked in one of the Livingston road gangs and on Friday night he drew his pay.

"I owe myself more money than I earned."

The flat statement admitted of no argument. It was a fact. He weighed the fact thoughtfully for as long as it took him to walk to the North Fork supermarket. That market had been beckoning to him since he first saw it. He entered and selected a wheeled basket, pushing it before him. He passed all of the products which needed refrigeration but he selected an accumulation of canned goods and two cans of coffee. He hesitated for a long two minutes before buying a whole ham.

"We've got to eat better than we've been eating," he said defensively.

When he presented the two sacks of groceries to Mother Maria Marthe her face tightened like one of her hands folding into a fist, more bone and skin than flesh, more contraction than expression. He had a

## The Lilies of the Field

startled impression that there were tears in her eyes but he could not be certain because she turned away so abruptly, the groceries in her arms.

"*Ach*, Schmidt!" she said.

The next day she was more annoying than ever, yelling "Schmidt!" at him when he was counseling with himself over his work, bothering his life with orders and suggestions and just plain interference. He decided that she was a natural henpecker and that he'd been foolish in his idea that she had softness in her.

"Hard as a hammer," he muttered. "Always beating on something."

He had, however, established a new pattern without thinking about it. Buying groceries seemed the natural thing to do when he had his second payday a week later and he engaged in no hesitations or arguments with himself.

"Mouths to feed," he said.

He rather liked the idea, liked the nuns and responded warmly to their obvious liking for himself. He enjoyed the English lessons and the Sunday music. Everything in his life seemed to fall into line, work and

*The Lilies of the Field*

more work, music, a little visiting, a little pondering, regular things to do at regular hours and no time to think about doing anything else.

The nuns worked all day in the fields as the weather grew warmer. He neither tried to understand their work nor to interfere with it. They were irrigating the land from a stream which fed into another puny stream that Westerners called a river. All that he knew about the irrigating process was that it was hard work. He had grown up in Columbia, South Carolina, and he was strictly city.

The idea of building a church obsessed him. He had no bricks but he laid floor when he had the foundation topped with cement. He used common lumber for his sub-floor and the best of his planks from the lumber pile for the surface. Some day, he thought, we'll maybe have money for linoleum or something. These planks won't take no polish.

He studied the church in Piedras every Sunday. There was not much to learn from it, but one feature of his own dream church baffled him. The brick chimney which had

## The Lilies of the Field

survived the fire stood high against the sky, higher than his projected roof. The fireplace and part of the stone mantel had survived, too, and that fireplace would be halfway down the right-hand side aisle of his church. He had never seen a church with a fireplace nor one with a chimney; that is, not a big chimney that called attention to itself.

Old Mother will probably have someone lay a log and sit herself in that warm spot come cold weather, he thought.

He tried to take it lightly but the chimney wasn't right. The church in Piedras had only a small hole near the altar side where a stovepipe would fit in winter, and it was a larger structure than his church. He could wreck the chimney, of course, but that old German, Gus Ritter, had built things to last. It would be difficult to get that chimney out of there with the equipment that he had. He did not like destroying something that had survived a disaster. That didn't seem right, either.

On a Tuesday in late July, the sad-faced man who ran the café in Piedras drove a beer truck up the road and parked behind

*The Lilies of the Field*

the station wagon. He had another man with him and neither man was friendly.

"The padre says to the people that you must have brick."

There were about five hundred adobe bricks in the truck and the two men made only a pretense of helping to unload it. Homer unloaded five bricks to their one.

"It is of no use," the sad-faced man said, "but we have brought it."

"Thanks."

Homer did not waste time talking to people who did not want to talk to him. He understood dimly the attitude of these people. It was the attitude of Orville Livingston. They saw no future for the nuns and they did not want to encourage what they did not approve. They did not want to be involved, or called upon for a succession of services, either.

Brick gave Homer a new impetus. He puddled adobe to use as mortar and he set his guide lines. He had done a little bricklaying but not much of it. This adobe brick was tricky. The bricks were uneven in size and crude. He had to socket his floor joists and he built a temporary wooden bracing

*The Lilies of the Field*

for his wall. He experimented and he worked slowly but, with the brick, the thing that he was creating became a reality.

He was leading three lives; the life of work in North Fork, the communal life of eating and singing with the nuns, the highly personal life of building a church. Mother Maria Marthe was a grimly irritating figure with her eternal "Schmidt!" and her interference, but most of the time he could block her out of his mind. When she annoyed him to the point where he could not block her out, he had spells of dark brooding during which he wondered why he was working harder than he had ever worked in his life, and for no pay; why he was staying here on this sun-baked prairie with so much world yet to see. It was a dull wonder, requiring no answer from him. The answer was before him. He was building a church.

He ran out of brick and, on a Monday night of full moon, life caught up with him.

It had been blazing, relentlessly hot for days and there was no moisture. Everything that he touched was hot and his

*The Lilies of the Field*

clothing clung to his skin; yet this was not a sweating heat like the heat of the South, it was a frying heat that skilleted a man, making his skin itch. There was a restlessness in his blood and in his nerves, a vague unhappiness clouding his thought. He sat with his back against the left-rear wheel of his station wagon and picked listlessly on his guitar. In the distance a coyote howled.

The cry was a high-pitched keening, a sound that climbed to a peak and broke. Homer lifted his head. The silver white of the moon lay over everything like snow. He felt along the strings for that coyote cry. He knew that he wouldn't find it, but he understood it.

He had heard coyotes before, almost every night. He was sensitive to animal tongue. He knew when a coyote was seeking a woman of his own kind. This coyote was not seeking that. He was finding the night unbearable because it was so big and so bright. He was lonely in it, feeling small and lost.

The cry rose again and another coyote answered. The other coyote was lonely,

## The Lilies of the Field

too, but the coyotes were not lonely for each other. It was bigger than that. Homer fingered the string on his guitar, then laid it down. He couldn't say what they were saying; he could only feel it. He straightened his body and stood, looking to the west where the coyotes were. There was nothing out there, nothing but wide, flat land and miserable little places like Piedras. He turned his body slowly so that he was facing east.

The mountains were a deep violet color slashed with silver. Everything was still. The hush had swallowed the last cry of the coyote and frightened him into joining the silence. Homer stretched his arms wide.

"Time to go," he said.

He returned his guitar to its case and climbed into the front seat of the station wagon. The noisy roar of the engine responding to the starter shattered the night, but there was an urgency in Homer Smith that ignored sound and silence now. He drove down the rutted road to the main highway and, as the car picked up speed, he relaxed under the wheel.

Over the pass, beyond the mountains,

*The Lilies of the Field*

lay the big city of the state. It had been a long time, too long a time! He could not tolerate nights so vast as this; he needed a city where people huddled together and kept one another warm. He sang softly as he drove and his car was a spinning reel on which the road wound up.

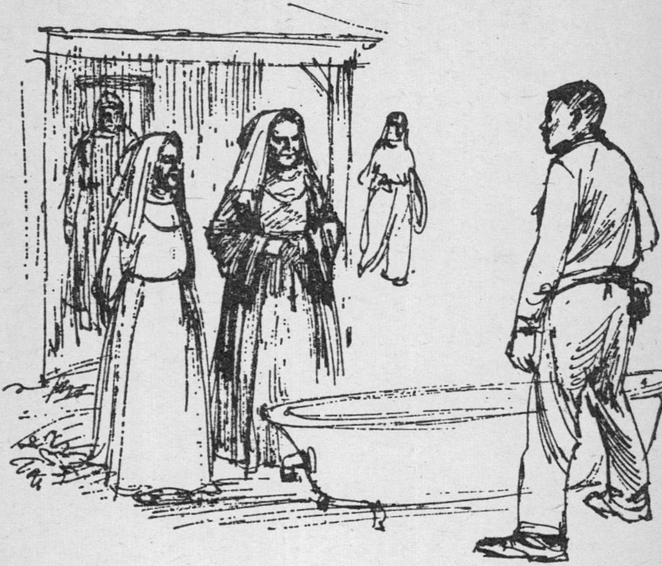

*chapter five*

The city was traffic-choked and noisy, and its lights were bright. The heat of summer rested on it like a cloud without rain, but a man could wet his throat with cold beer in the daytime and mingle with his own kind at night, eating and drinking whatever he found. He could listen to loud, rhythmic sound from juke boxes and dance with women and laugh at jokes. He could look into the eyes of women and see himself there, feeling pride in his manhood. He could stand big in his body with gray fog in his mind and hear his own blood running in his veins. He could go to the Baptist church on Sunday and sing hymns that his mother and his father sang before he was born, weeping a little because he had been a sinner all week. He could leave the church with all the sin washed out of him, feeling clean.

Homer Smith loved all of it, the standing tall and the falling down. Most of all, he

## The Lilies of the Field

liked the speech of men and women like himself, and the humor of them. A man heard no funny stories from people of another language who could not speak English well, and he could tell no funny stories. Humor belonged to the language that a man knew. He liked companionship and his room in the boardinghouse, and the bathroom down the hall where he could bathe in a tub instead of showering himself from a bucket. He liked the hard feel of pavement under his feet, the odor of cooking food that floated out of strange windows and doorways, the children who were in constant motion around him. He liked the sirens of police, fire, and hospital vehicles, the bright exteriors of taverns and the twilight dimness within. This was the city.

The nuns and a town named Piedras and the Livingston Construction Company belonged to a hazy dream, as unreal as incidents in the life of another man. He never sat down deliberately to think about them and such stray memories as floated in and out of his mind did not disturb him. His life in the Army was gone, too, to be re-

*The Lilies of the Field*

called only through conscious effort and not worth that. He lived in what he had, and with what he had, finding life good.

His money ran low in ten days and he went to work for a wrecking company. His first job was with a crew that was wrecking a carbarn no longer used by the tramway company. It was heavy, dirty, dangerous work, with much steel to handle and grime over everything. The next job, by comparison, was easy. A half-block of houses had to come down to create a blank which could be converted into a parking lot. They were small and old, low-rent houses, known in the South as row houses but in the West as terraces; houses all alike, built together wall to wall. Everything that could be stripped by hand was stripped, then a crane, with a big metal ball, knocked the walls down. The job took three days.

On the third day, Homer was sorting through the salvage, stacking the theoretically usable doors, window frames and fixtures. There were sinks, basins, eight bathtubs. He piled the bathtubs, then stood looking at them, hearing in his mind a high,

*The Lilies of the Field*

clear call as compelling as a coyote's cry to the moon.

"Those girls need a bathtub," he said.

It was the first time he had consciously thought about the nuns and they were suddenly alive in his mind. He had seen them hauling buckets of water from the well in the evening, many buckets, and he had seen how crude everything was about the house. Gus Ritter, that old German farmer, had been a tight-fisted man. He didn't improve a place except where it paid him.

The foreman was a big man, almost as big as Homer was. Homer sought him out. "How's to buy one of those tubs?" he said.

"Sure enough? You want your own personal tub, boy?"

"How much?"

"You could steal it and nobody would care. That kind is no good. You got some way to haul it?"

"Yes."

"Okay. Give me two bucks to keep it honest."

Homer gave him the two dollars. He saw the bills go into the foreman's pocket and

*The Lilies of the Field*

he knew that the company would never see those bills. That didn't matter. He'd bought what he wanted at the price asked. The bathtubs were high and narrow, standing on dragon feet. He picked the best one of them. It wouldn't go into the station wagon so he upended it on the top, the feet pointing skyward, lashing it in place with rope. The bathroom windows had been removed intact, small windows of red, yellow, and green glass in diamond pattern. He bought two of them from the foreman for a dollar each and, with the purchase, a vision returned, haunting him.

He drew his pay at the end of the day and headed for the hills.

It was afternoon on Friday when he drove into familiar territory. He stayed on the highway when it looped around North Fork. The crops were prospering under a bright sun; potatoes, wheat, barley, lettuce, cauliflower. The hazy blue mountains were on his right. Within a few miles the fields on his left became bleak, sage, and greasewood, sprinkled with a few indomitable flowers of blue, yellow, and

*The Lilies of the Field*

pink. A hawk floated low, gliding on motionless wings, and a rabbit scurried across the road.

Homer drove over a small bridge and the stream below it was a thin trickle. He turned to his right on a rutted road and the nuns were in the field, working on their variegated crop, fighting for their growing stuff against weeds and voracious insects and the parched dryness of the soil. It was good to see them again, but he did not slow down nor look in their direction. He was not certain of his reception and he was willing to defer it. He parked in his accustomed spot and sat looking at his unfinished church.

Nobody had disturbed it and no one had brought bricks with which to complete it. It had a desolate look; one wall built as high as a man's shoulder, the others low; the chimney pointing upward like the skeleton finger of a giant. There was an untidy scattering of rubble on the ground. Homer got the scoop shovel from the barn toolroom and started shoveling. He cleared the area and dug a hole with his spade into which he tumbled the debris.

## The Lilies of the Field

The bell rang and he straightened. Old Mother never rang the bell for the nuns because they knew when to come for meals. That bell was for him. He laid the spade aside, carried his bucket to the well, washed his hands and walked into the house. They were waiting for him, standing in their places at the table, just as if he had never been away. He bowed his head while they prayed. When he looked up after the "Amen" they were all looking at him happily. Nobody said anything but they were glad that he was home. A man felt a thing like that. Nobody had to say anything.

There was an omelet and coarse bread, but there were vegetables, too, fresh vegetables. The farm was starting to pay off.

They resumed the English lessons after supper and Homer's ear was sharper because he had been away. They were doing better with the language but he could hear the soft echo of South Carolina coming back to him when they spoke.

Better than a phonograph accent, he thought. Used to be you could hear the turntable going around when they spoke anything in English.

*The Lilies of the Field*

He did not unveil the bathtub until after breakfast the next day. He drove the station wagon close to the house and eased the tub down from the top. He called old Mother out to see it. Sisters Gertrud and Albertine came with her. He made an awkward gesture toward the tub, not naming it. After all, these were girls who built a high fence around the privy.

"A present," he said.

He was facing Mother Maria Marthe. Her eyes squinted as though she found the sun too bright. "*Das ist gut,* Schmidt," she said, "*Das ist gut.*"

She said something in German to the two nuns and went hurriedly into the house. Homer did not have to explain to her that he needed a place in which to install the tub. When she returned, she led him to a pantry off the kitchen. This was the deepest penetration that he had made into the nuns' quarters. He had not even known that the pantry existed.

"Here," she said.

It was a small room but that was her problem. He hauled the tub in and set it on

## The Lilies of the Field

its feet. He had taken some pipe as a necessary accessory to the tub and he had bought a secondhand blowtorch in the city. He cut a hole in the floor where it met the wall and angled the pipe through it, attaching it to the drain pipe of the tub and soldering it in place. He put the rubber plug in the drain and the tub was in business. He dug a trench outside the house to run the water off. They would still have to haul water because he couldn't give them a pump and a plumbing job, but this was something. He felt good about it.

He still lacked bricks, so he settled down to carpentry, making pews and kneelers like those in the church at Piedras. He lacked a lathe and he had to work with what he had, so the pews were mere benches without polish or curlicues, but he built them solidly and the day passed swiftly.

"Old Mother's got to pray me some bricks," he said softly. "If she doesn't, she's wasting my time."

He sat at the counter in Piedras while the nuns were at Mass on Sunday. He or-

## The Lilies of the Field

dered his big breakfast. The sad-looking man broke eggs into the skillet and surrounded them with bacon.

"It is not reasonable that you have come back," he said.

"It makes sense to me."

"It could not. Everybody says that you are gone and this is how it had to be. They laugh at the nuns because the nuns say that you will return."

Homer's body stiffened. "I don't want to see nobody laughing at those nuns."

"This they know." The man cast a wary eye at his big customer. "Now nobody will laugh."

"No. That's right. Nobody's going to laugh."

"The padre says to them that you will return."

"How did he know?"

"That Mother Superior, she told him."

"How did she know?"

"She knew."

Homer drank his coffee, savoring the fine aroma of bacon. He had not known, himself, that he would ever come back. He had not given it a thought. How could old

## The Lilies of the Field

Mother know? He had a dark suspicion that it had something to do with her praying. She had never got it out of her head that God had given Homer Smith to her. If that was a fact, she'd be certain that he couldn't wander off. He belonged to her. That was something Homer had never liked. The idea of belonging to someone stirred a racial antagonism in him. No Negro was ever going to belong to anybody again. Not ever! He was free.

The breakfast was good and he ate it. The idea of freedom moved around in his mind while he ate, not moving in a worrisome way, merely in a curious manner. It was a strange thing, freedom. He had been free in the city. Nobody told him to do anything. He kept his own hours, ate when he wanted to eat, slept as late as he liked. Here, old Mother was always ringing bells or yelling "Schmidt" or telling him to do something. She exploded inside of herself if he didn't get up at bird-waking time. She was so certain about owning him that she never said "thank you" for anything. Not one time had she said "thank you."

*The Lilies of the Field*

"The padre, that Father Gomez, he will be very happy that you have come back to those nuns," the man behind the counter said.

"Why should he be happy?"

"He will say that it proves a religious thing."

"What religious thing?"

"Faith. It is a word for what is unreasonable. If a man believes in an unreasonable thing, that is faith. It is not reasonable that you should come back to this place and work for nothing. Nobody believed it. You have come back."

Homer ate contentedly. That was an interesting idea. He liked interesting ideas. Faith was what old Mother had. She believed that he would come back. She believed that he could build a church all by himself, maybe even without bricks. That wasn't a reasonable idea. He hadn't ever built anything all by himself. He was free, building that church, just as free as he was in the city, even more so. There wasn't anybody else to build it. He didn't need any wages. He had a full life. He had

## The Lilies of the Field

many things. He was free like the lilies of the field. It was a strange thing. As this Spanish man said, it wasn't reasonable.

"Me," the man said. "I have no faith. I do not believe in the Church. I do not go to the Mass."

Homer looked at him with interest. "I don't know what that does for you," he said. "All those other Spanish are in there sitting on those benches or doing whatever they do at Mass, not working. You're over here, working, fixing my breakfast."

"It is reasonable. You pay me. I make money."

"I never saw another customer in here during the Mass. Unless you get a hungry Baptist in your place, you don't make money."

"So, I sit here and do nothing. It is a reasonable thing. No priest tells me what to do."

The first stragglers were coming out of the church. Homer rose and paid for his breakfast. The man behind the counter baffled him in a mild way but he was not interested in him. The man could stay just

*The Lilies of the Field*

as he was, where he was, being reasonable. If the man ever got faith, Sunday was going to be a hungry day in Piedras.

The nuns, as usual, were the last ones out of the church. Homer amused himself, looking big and dangerous beside the station wagon, frowning at all of these people who had laughed at his nuns, seeing them turn quickly away from him. He did not frown at Father Gomez who came out with old Mother. The priest was smiling and he extended his hand.

"It is nice to see you again," he said. "I believe that you will have a surprise or two this week, Señor Smith." He turned his head. "Don't you agree, Mother Superior?"

Mother Maria Marthe either understood, or sensed, what he was saying. She nodded and, amazingly, for the first time since Homer Smith had known her, she smiled.

"*Ja*," she said.

The surprise was not long in developing. Early Monday morning, vehicles of various types and ages arrived at Homer's working area. Each vehicle brought adobe

## The Lilies of the Field

bricks and each driver had approximately the same speech.

"I am happy to bring these bricks for the chapel. I have had in my heart a doubt of you and I am sorry."

After his astonishment at the first two versions of the speech, Homer adjusted cheerfully to the situation. Old Padre must have preached hell to these Spanish, he thought. Wish I could have heard it.

The bricks piled up and he went to work again. The day climaxed with the beer truck and the largest donation of the day, five hundred bricks. The driver, a wide-shouldered, husky, embarrassed man made the set approach. His companion, the sad man from the café, spat at a grasshopper, missing him.

"I have come only to see this thing," he said. "I have brought no bricks."

Homer shrugged. It made no difference. This man probably did not believe in bricks. It was not reasonable that all of these bricks should be here, so they were not. The broad-shouldered man laughed. Now that he had made his speech, he was

*The Lilies of the Field*

no longer embarrassed. He slapped his companion on the back and walked around the partially built chapel, shaking his head

"You do not know well the adobe," he said.

"I'm learning."

"You should have help."

Homer resented him and he was glad to see him go. A shadow had fallen on his church which everyone else called a chapel. Now that these Spanish were bringing bricks they were going to tell him what to do and how to do it. That could not be. He had to finish it as he had begun it. It was his church. For the first time since he started work on the project, he worried. Mother Maria Marthe added to his worry. She walked around his bricks, making clucking noises like a hen that has just laid something; owning his bricks as she owned him, acting like she'd prayed them into existence.

If I hadn't come back, there wouldn't be no bricks, he thought sullenly.

Old Mother was oblivious. "Schmidt," she said. "Dese people vill help you. All iss vell."

*The Lilies of the Field*

"I don't want any help."

His mind was set on that point and when helpful neighbors came to watch and make suggestions, he was curtly hostile. They brought no brick on Tuesday or on Wednesday but men with time to spare from whatever they did normally, came in person. Some of them wanted to lay bricks and all of them were mouth experts, telling him what he should do. They were very friendly about it. When he wouldn't let them work, they sat and smoked, watching him and sometimes shaking their heads, making remarks to one another in Spanish.

They ain't commenting on how good I'm doing neither, he thought.

Thursday bothered him. He did not know whether he would still have a job with Livingston Construction Company and he was reluctant to leave his own job unguarded. There wasn't any sense in telling old Mother to chase these Spanish because she liked the idea of having them do some of the work. She didn't understand how he felt about it. All that she cared about was getting her chapel-church built. She didn't care who built it.

*The Lilies of the Field*

Homer made two signs and placed them conspicuously on his walls. One read KEEP OFF! and the other was equally uncompromising: DON'T TOUCH ANYTHING! He drove off then to North Fork.

Orville Livingston's eyebrows moved upward and his jaw moved forward when he saw Homer Smith. "Where have you been?" he said.

"Vacation."

"Yeah? Why did you come back?"

"Had to finish my church."

"Are you going to finish it?"

"I'll finish it. Right now I'm gaining on my brick."

"Humph. Well, they ought to read you out of the Baptist Church but I'm glad you're back. I'm short-handed."

Homer went out on a road gang and Livingston had not exaggerated his short-handedness. The work was heavy. Thursday night Homer checked his church and no one had disturbed it. Friday night, with his two days pay, he loaded up on groceries, enjoying the adventure of pushing his cart through the supermarket again and selecting what he wanted. When he reached

## The Lilies of the Field

home and presented his sacks to old Mother, she shook her head at him.

"*Nein*, Schmidt," she said. "No more."

She showed him vegetables in jars which the nuns had canned for winter eating, fresh vegetables ready for the table, an entire new generation of chickens in the fowl run ready to be thinned out. He had been blind to all that. He experienced an odd twinge of disappointment.

"That's fine," he said. "That's just fine."

He had never been vitally interested in what the nuns did, or how. He knew that they worked hard and that was all that he cared to know. Now they had something to show for their work. They didn't need his groceries any more. He walked across the clearing to his church. The Spanish had been interfering in his absence. They had built a big mortar box with some of his old lumber. He sat and smoked, taking counsel with himself.

There was a way of spreading adobe on the outside of the brick and smoothing it out, a little like stone. He had studied the church in Piedras and he believed that he knew how it was done, but he had never

*The Lilies of the Field*

seen anyone do it. These Spanish planned to do it for his church. That's why they built that box to do their puddling. He resented any and every hand laid on that church other than his own, but he told himself that this was a practical matter and that the Spanish knew how to do this work.

"No sense in me getting sore," he said.

Some intangible thing, some joyful spirit, had gone out of his life and he tried to call it back. He sang as he laid brick on Saturday and he was friendly to the Spanish people who came out to watch him, so friendly that he surprised them. They got in his way, trying to help him. No one attempted to mix adobe clay; everyone wanted to help lay brick.

"No!" he said. " I got my ideas. I got to do it my way."

"*Como?* There is only one way to lay the brick."

They did not understand his attitutde and he had taken a positive stand at an awkward time. He had reached the point in one wall that called for the installation of a window, high up and placed, as in the church at Piedras, so that light would fall

## The Lilies of the Field

on the altar. He had the window intact in its frame, a small window that need never be opened. It was not easy to set it properly in place with the bricks holding it firm. He had measured his space carefully, but he had difficulty when he tried to set it. A short, thin man named Juan Archuleta joined him on his working platform.

"It is a matter of aggravation, this," Juan Archuleta said. "I have done it."

He broke a brick deftly, scarcely seeming to glance at it but breaking it to the exact size that he wanted. He wedged pieces into place and he spread his adobe mortar. He knew how to set a window and Homer grudgingly admitted it. The little man took no credit for what he did and made no point of it. He talked as he worked.

"I like how you sing," he said.

"A man works better singing."

"*Si*. Singing is good. You like guitar?"

"Got one of my own."

"*Bueno*. You come to my house tonight for the dinner. Drink a little, sing a little, play the guitar."

"Sounds good."

A man couldn't stay hostile to another

*The Lilies of the Field*

man who helped him work and who invited him to dinner. "I have worked much with adobe," Juan Archuleta said. "It is the stuff of this country."

He helped Homer with the twin window on the other wall and he backed him up in telling the other men that two workers on the bricks were enough. Without making a point of it, he worked over a couple of trouble spots where the wall met the chimney and enclosed the fireplace.

"You work smooth," Homer said grudgingly.

"A little work. *De nada*. You have worked much. I could not do so much. I am not a strong man."

Homer shook his head. This Jaun Archuleta was easy to like; man with honey on his tongue. He met Juan's wife and his children and his neighbors. He drank white liquor that he could feel in the roots of his hair like electricity and he sang songs for his new friends. He ate food that was hotter than the liquor but strangely satisfying and he listened to songs that he had never heard before in a language that he did not understand.

*The Lilies of the Field*

"*Adios, Mariquita linda,
Yo me voy
Porque tú ya no me quieres
Como yo to quiero a ti.*"

He admired it. It had sadness but no misery. He could pick it up on the guitar and play along with it but he could not sing it as he sang Latin with the nuns. This language did not break down to sounds that he could carry in his head or shape with his mouth. On the faster, more cheerful music it was easier. He could make a lot of *ya-ya-ya* sounds that were almost Spanish even if they didn't mean anything.

Homer did not know when the party ended; it tapered off slowly. He rode home in Juan Archuleta's old car, singing. There was a silvery whiteness over the land, a chill in the air. He chuckled foolishly as he stood beside his station wagon watching Juan drive away. A dozen impressions of the evening whirled around in his mind but the one that rose to the surface was inconsequential.

"Those Spanish have a way with beans," he said. "Make them taste like food."

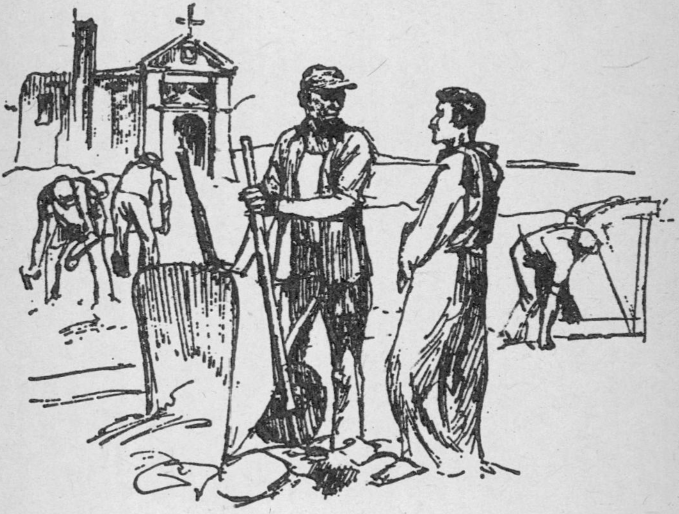

## chapter six

A Livingston Construction Company truck delivered a thousand bricks on Monday morning. There was no message, no explanation offered. There did not have to be.

"Old man lost a bet with himself," Homer said. "He bet I wouldn't ever do this work. He bet I would be long gone by now."

The new bricks were far superior to any that Homer had laid; regular brickyard adobe, uniform in size and quality. It did not seem right to lay them on the upper levels with the inferior bricks below. The adobe coating, of course, would hide them but Homer considered tearing out the front of the church and using the new bricks there. He didn't mind the work but he decided against it. The people who had brought him bricks when he needed them had a right to have their bricks in the church where they were put.

He had more bricks now than he had

*The Lilies of the Field*

hoped for and he decided to build his church higher. That would change the proportions but it would be more impressive. He had a driving urgency in him, a sense of time that he had not had earlier. Time had not mattered; now it did. He did not try to reason why.

The helpful Spanish brought him logs for his roof beams and they were more of a problem than ever. They were his friends and they were all over the place. Whatever they should be doing to make a living was obviously being neglected, but his blunt query—"Shouldn't you be doing something else somewhere?"—brought only shrugs and grins. They had developed a religious fervor and the finishing of the church had become important to them. They refused to accept the idea that it was his church.

"Look!" he said. "You fellows build an altar. I don't know about such things. If this chapel-church has got to have statues in it, you fix it about them. You let these bricks alone!"

They built an altar within his church while he was laying the long beams across

*The Lilies of the Field*

the walls with two feet of log projecting on either side as in the Piedras church. He laid board across the beams and, at this point, Juan Archuleta insisted upon helping him again. Together they coated the boards thickly with adobe mud. Juan helped, too, with the adobe plaster on the inside walls of the church itself.

The approach of Thursday posed a problem. If he went to work for Orville Livingston there would be no one to control the Spanish. There was no longer any purpose in his work for Livingston. The nuns didn't need groceries any more.

The man sent you all those bricks, his conscience said.

"No. He didn't. He didn't send me anything. I gave him work for wages. He sent those bricks to old Mother. Ashamed of how he said 'no' to her."

With that settled, he continued to work on the church. On Thursday afternoon, Father Gomez came out to see it. He walked all around it, making pleasant comments, then went to see Mother Maria Marthe. She came to where Homer was working after the priest left. He was white-

*The Lilies of the Field*

washing the interior and he did not want to stop.

"Schmidt," she said. "I talk to you."

"*Ja*," he said.

It was his way of kidding her when she annoyed him. She sat on one of his pews and motioned for him to sit beside her.

"It is finish—nearly—der shapel," she said.

"Almost."

She nodded, her eyes momentarily closed. "*Ja. Gott ist gutt*, Schmidt. Sunday, Father Gomez say Mass in dis shapel, der first Mass. You vill sit dere. Der front pew."

She pointed to the space before the altar where the pew had not yet been placed. She seemed very happy, very proud. She was, Homer knew, trying to do something for him, give him an honor; but his Baptist soul recoiled at the thought of sitting up front, in the first pew or any pew, at a Catholic Mass. He looked at her and he couldn't take her happiness away or do anything to hurt her.

"That will be nice," he said.

He resumed his work with even greater

*The Lilies of the Field*

urgency when she left him, understanding more clearly the sense of time that drove him. He joked with the Spanish, he ate with the nuns, he continued the English lessons after supper; but only half of him did these things, the other half listened always to the ticking of an invisible clock.

On Saturday, not even the Spanish could find much to do. Homer used them in the clean-up, the removal and stacking of lumber that had been used for scaffolding, the break-up of mortar boxes, the leveling of ground. This was not very interesting so by early afternoon the Spanish had all left. Homer finished the policing himself, cleaning and leveling and removing trash.

He sat, then, smoking a cigarette and looking at his church. He had done it. Old Mother had said; "Build me a chapel-church." He had built it. He had not known how to do it, he had had no plans, adobe was a new stuff in his life—but there it was! His church stood strong with blue sky behind it, a church with angles that would be stiff and harsh in wood, soft in abode. It had a pediment that he had made in place above the door with a crucifix at

*The Lilies of the Field*

the peak. He rose and walked inside, glad to be alone.

The sunlight flowed through two windows that had come out of row-house bathrooms. The light took color from the diamonds in the panes and spilled that color on the whitewashed walls. The church in Piedras lacked this cathedral touch; it had only plain glass. His pews were in place and he walked down the aisle. He stood with his back to the altar and looked at the places where the five nuns would sit. His throat felt tight and he had no thoughts at all. He walked hurriedly down the aisle and out into the sunlight.

A flight of birds flew overhead. They were flying high and heading south. It was September and his spring was gone, and his summer. Another flight of birds passed over and he watched them out of sight.

Those birds got a message, he thought. A man ought to have as much sense as a bird.

The bell summoned him to supper and old Mother was feeling festive tonight. She had put a couple of her chickens in the pot and there was chicken stew. All the

## The Lilies of the Field

nuns seemed excited and happy. They had a chapel-church of their own and a priest coming to say Mass in the morning. It didn't seem like a night for English lessons. Homer brought his guitar in and played for them. He played some of the Spanish music that he remembered, not trying to sing it.

*"Adios, Mariquita linda. . . ."*

He played some of his own music, too, and he sang that: "Water Boy" and "Shenandoah" and "Deep River." He started playing the Latin music and Sister Albertine sang, bringing the others in. He sang Latin sounds with them and it was a happy evening, better than the night with the Spanish.

He sat for a long time beside the station wagon after the nuns had retired. He told himself that he should have said "good-by" to old Mother, but it wasn't his way to put his feelings into words. Old Mother looked into a man's heart and she had an understanding mind. When he was gone, nobody would have to tell her anything; she would just know.

He'd like to say a word to Sister Alber-

*The Lilies of the Field*

tine, too. He'd like to tell her that he liked her singing. She wasn't so strong as the other nuns, Sister Albertine, but she did delicate things that a man liked. She was the one who drew the picture of the wooden church that he couldn't ever build. She had made pictures of him, too. Somebody sent her a package from Germany with pencils and brushes and paper and paint. He hadn't seen her paint anything but she'd made a lot of pictures of him with her pencils when he was singing or talking English at the nuns or working on the church. Better than a camera, she was. He had one of the pictures of himself that she gave him. It was signed with her name. Saying good-by to her wasn't something that he could do, either.

He looked long at his church, then he went inside. It was filled with silent shadow except where starlight filtered through his small windows. He walked down the aisle and he knew that there was something that he wanted to say to God about this church. He knelt in one of the pews and he lifted up his heart, but no words came. It wasn't

*The Lilies of the Field*

something that he could talk about, not even to God.

A rabbit bounded across the clearing when he came out of the church. It vanished and no other night creature moved or spoke. It was deep night, a late hour, and that was the best time.

The starter awakened the engine of the station wagon to noisy life and a touch of the switch sent a flow of light down the rutted road. Homer Smith drove that road to the highway and he knew that he was never coming back. A man couldn't roam forever, nor pleasure himself in strange cities indefinitely. There was a settling-down time at the end of all that. The road was lonely and he sang softly to himself as he drove.

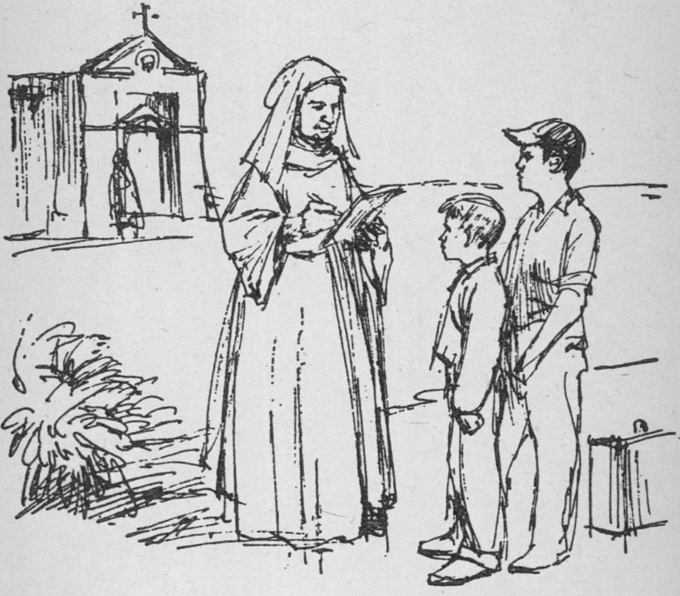

## chapter seven

The legend of Homer Smith came into being within twenty-four hours of his disappearance from the scene of his labors. Father Gomez spoke feelingly of him and a Methodist named Orville Livingston came to see the chapel that he had not believed would be built. The newspaper in North Fork ran a story with a photograph of the chapel. Because that chapel is unique in appearance and history, a reporter from the state's largest newspaper made the trip to Piedras and interviewed many people who were eager to talk of its building. Every Spanish-American in the region claimed to have known Homer Smith well, and they are a people who like tales of saints who walk the earth and of angels that take men unaware.

A man named Juan Archuleta swore that he had laid bricks beside Homer Smith and that often the bricks flew into place with no one touching them. Another man named

## The Lilies of the Field

José Gonzalez, who owned a café in Piedras, claimed that he was the intimate and the closest confidant of the chapel builder, that often a white light shone around the man and that, on one occasion, Homer Smith said to him: "God sent me to this place to build a church and to make these nuns famous. When I have done this thing you will see me no more."

Mother Maria Marthe and her nuns were reticent, reluctant to speak for publication about Homer Smith. That very reticence drew them into the legend and created curiosity. People wrote to them and sent them money, soliciting prayers. Orville Livingston, a Rotarian, was invited to speak to the Capital City Rotarians about his experience with Homer Smith and the nuns after he had spoken to his own group in North Fork. Publicity created more publicity and tourists journeyed to a section of the state which they had never seen because they were told that an unusual experience awaited them, that here was a modern shrine.

No one can explian these things. The aim of Mother Maria Marthe was publi-

## The Lilies of the Field

cized with the rest of the story and substantial sums of money were contributed to help her realize her aim.

Today there are several fine buildings and four new nuns under the direction of the aging Mother Superior. The buildings have electricity and modern plumbing. There are boys from broken homes, and boys who have been in difficulty with the law, studying in the classrooms, working in the fields and in the workshops. They have made their school a noted institution by their loyalty to it. The school is growing in public esteem and in facilities for service to Spanish-American young people who are easy to neglect because they are difficult to understand.

The chapel occupies the key position, with the other buildings grouped in an arc around it. It is a favorite subject of photographers and one may buy postcards of its exterior and interior in Piedras or in North Fork. Three prominent artists have painted it and one of the paintings hangs in the State Museum of Art. There is no chapel like it anywhere. It is of conventional adobe but some trick of proportion makes it memorable. There is strength in its lines and an indefinable grace. A voluble and oft-quoted sculptress has described it as "a true primitive," whatever that means. The chimney, of course, is its really distinctive feature; a brick chimney designed for a two-story house, rising above the flat-roofed adobe chapel like a steeple.

There is a fireplace halfway down the right-hand aisle of the chapel. It is a tradition with the nuns to burn logs in the fireplace on Sundays during the cold weather. The hardier tourists of the fall and winter season consider this a charming touch.

Mother Maria Marthe has grown older. Her English has improved but she still struggles with the "w" and the "th," although the struggle is scarcely apparent in the speeches that she has memorized. She is at her best when she performs her favorite task; the guiding of tourists through the buildings, climaxing always with the chapel. There is, as in the speech of several other nuns, a touch of the South in her voice, a soft slurring, an odd emphasis on certain syllables.

She directs attention first to the oil painting on the wall in the rear of the chapel. It is the painting of a powerful Negro with large features and widely spaced eyes. His head is thrown back in an attitude of exhortation, or, perhaps, of song, his lips parted to reveal two perfect rows of teeth. There is a nimbus of light around the man's head.

"This is the chapel of Saint Benedict the Moor," Mother Maria Marthe says. "That painting of the saint is the work of Sister Albertine. The model was a man named Schmidt who came to us under the direction of God. He built this chapel with his two hands under great difficulties. It is all from him."

She pauses then and her voice drops. "He was not of our faith, nor of our skin," she says, "but he was a man of greatness, of an utter devotion."

7-66

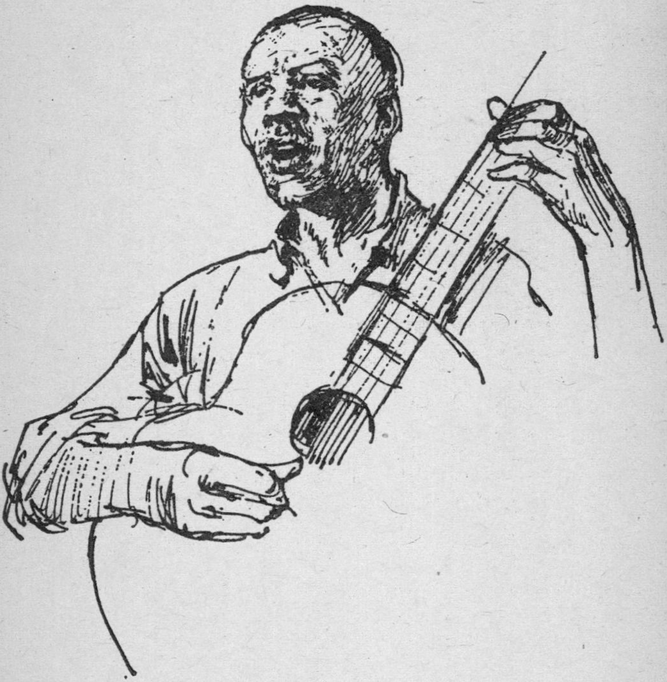